THIS JOURNAL BELONGS TO

www.ingramcontent.com/pod-product-compliance
Lightning Source LLC
Chambersburg PA
CBHW030720220526
45463CB00005B/2134
9781690131137